AF815394

Estate Planning for Beginners

A Guide for Protecting Your Loved Ones and Leaving a Legacy They Will Always Cherish.

By E. Lawrence Brock

Attorney & Counselor at Law

Published by E. Lawrence Brock

193 S 100 E, St. George, UT 84770

www.estateplandesigner.com

Interior Book Design by Brian Coates

Edited by Amy Jones

Cover photos by Matsumi Kat

This book is dedicated to my firstborn son, Ryan, who as a toddler sat next to me as I listened to law school tapes in the car for hours on the California freeways. His untimely death as a young, married man changed the way I see my purpose in life.

I also dedicate this book to my loyal and supportive wife, Joyce, who has stood by me with love and encouragement through the best of times and through the worst of times.

Joyce, my life is yours; thank you.

Table of Contents

Foreword

For years, I've witnessed Larry's commitment and dedication to his clients as he's helped them design estate plans and settle estates. When a 2010 a California Lawyer magazine featured the founders of LegalZoom with the headline, "Will These Guys Put You Out of Business?" Larry believed the real question should be, "Will These Guys Hurt The Public?" Larry has often expressed concern over incorrect estate planning and how it can harm families.

In response to services like LegalZoom, Larry has devoted countless hours and resources to creating a process that combines the best of the DIY legal movement with the expertise of qualified lawyers. He's discovered how to use the Internet to combine education, estate plan design tools, and individual attorney offices to ensure that the public doesn't have to sacrifice low quality legal services in exchange for online convenience. This book is Larry's first step in his mission to revolutionize estate planning.

Joanna Averett, CFP, AEP
Vice President and Wealth Advisor, First American Trust
President, National Association of Estate Planning Councils, 2012 - 2013

Introduction:
Bilbo Baggins

Have you ever heard of a Hobbit named Bilbo Baggins? He was an expert at estate planning. When Bilbo celebrated his 111th birthday in the book Fellowship of the Ring, he knew he would be leaving Hobbiton forever. Rather than abandon his poor nephew Frodo to deal with all the legal kerfuddles that would happen after he left, Bilbo placed all the necessary estate documents on the mantle and kindly told Gandalf the wizard where they were. He even set aside gifts for his Hobbit friends that were properly labeled and had personal notes of farewell.

When Bilbo's unfriendly cousins came to claim what they thought was theirs, Frodo could have been facing years of lawsuits. Luckily for him, Bilbo's documents were precise, correct, and followed the legal rules of Hobbiton to the letter. After looking over the carefully drafted will, the unfriendly cousins couldn't even argue about Frodo keeping the house. The only thing they could do was leave in a huff, much to Frodo's relief.

Bilbo wasn't a particularly rich Hobbit; he only had a house and the bits and pieces he'd collected over the years. Many would have thought he didn't even need an estate plan. But without it, his house could have been torn apart by squabbling relatives.

By planning ahead and preparing his estate documents clearly and correctly, Bilbo saved his nephew from years of lawsuits and some very nasty arguments. Not only did he secure his financial assets and protect them from his unfriendly relatives, but he also preserved a legacy in the gifts he gave to his friends.

Bilbo did the four essential actions of Estate Planning:

1. He prepared estate-planning documents ahead of time
2. He made sure that all the documents were filled out and signed correctly according to Hobbit law.

3. He properly labeled gifts of personal property and left behind notes for his friends and family.
4. Finally, he told someone he trusted where to find his estate documents and left them in a place where they were easily accessible.

Although the book series *Lord of the Rings* is fiction, the message it sends about estate planning applies to anyone 18 years old or older. No one knows when tragedy will strike or when Hobbit uncles will suddenly disappear. Whether you have a mansion, a modest home, or just a bunch of items in a beat-up duffle bag, everyone needs an estate plan.

Is it a bird? Is it a plane? Or is it a pile of useless papers?

Chapter 1: Okay, I Need One...But What Is It?

Simply put, an estate plan is a set of instructions. These instructions explain what will happen to your possessions after you die. But estate plans aren't only for when you die; they can also to leave instructions for what happens if you are in a coma, disappear, or become incapacitated.

When you have an estate plan, YOU are in charge of the following decisions:

- How your money is used
- Who makes health care decisions about you if you can't make them yourself
- Whether or not you should be disconnected from life support
- Who raises your minor children if you are unable to do so
- Who receives your financial assets and personal property

Fortunately, YOU can make all of these decisions and preserve a lasting legacy for your heirs if you take the initiative and create a strong estate plan.

How to Use This Book

This book is a manual, NOT an actual estate plan. The worksheets at the end of the chapters are there to help you gather all the information you'll need for your estate plan, but they are not legal documents. Besides giving you information about estate planning, the worksheets will help you keep track of the decisions you'll need to make. This book will guide and educate you through your journey so that when your lawyer starts talking gobbledygook, you'll understand what he's saying and you'll be able to design the best estate plan possible. There are two ways to use this book:

1. Fill out the worksheets at the end of the chapters to gather all the information you need. Take that information to a qualified attorney so that together, you can design the estate plan that is best for you.

Many lawyers have estate plan packages available, but may not offer the documents needed for your particular situation. After you read this book, you'll know what to ask for.

2. Or, you can use this book to gather the information you need, then submit that information to www.estateplandesigner.com. If you don't have time to visit with a lawyer face to face, this website sends your information to a member of the Academy of Online Estate Planning Attorneys and they will draft an estate plan tailored to your specific needs.

With option 2, you can drastically reduce the cost of creating an estate plan by submitting your information online, but still have your estate plan drafted by a professional attorney.

Let's get started!

It's sweet that Grandma told me I get everything when she dies, but it'll be so much nicer when her wishes are documented, signed, and witnessed.

Chapter 2: What Estate Planning Documents Do I Need?

Ever heard of Terri Schiavo? She's the young woman who was kept alive on life support for 15 years even though she was completely brain dead. Before the heart attack that landed her in a coma, Terri had said she didn't want medical heroics if tragedy struck. Unfortunately, she never documented those wishes.

Tragedies like this happen all the time because people don't have the proper paperwork.

To avoid a similar fate, you MUST take action and put your wishes in writing via an estate plan. But which documents do you need?

The following is a list of standard estate planning documents. If your attorney doesn't offer some of these documents in your estate plan, you'll know which ones to ask for. Most people understand they need a will, but never realize that emergency medical documents are also an important part of an estate plan. Make sure you have ALL of the documents that you need.

Basic Estate Planning Documents

Will

A will describes how you want your property distributed after death. It also appoints guardians for minor children and appoints a personal representative to carry out the instructions of the will and distribute your assets after your death (i.e. an "executor"). This document only comes into effect after death.

If some of your children are minors, a will is one of the most important documents you can create because in it you appoint guardians to raise your children, if you cannot raise them yourself.

When you name the desired guardians of your children, you can also make it clear whom you do NOT want as guardians of your children.

If you don't make these decisions in a properly documented will, then the state will make those decisions for you.

Everyone age 18 and older needs a will.

Trusts

Imagine your 16-year-old son came up to you and said, "Can I have $10,000?" Even if you had enough money to give it to him, would you do it? Just like that? As a parent, you'd want to know the money would be invested in worthy pursuits, not wasted on parties, vacations, or drugs.

When you give away money in a will, you're handing over a lump sum with no questions asked. If you're worried about how your heirs (i.e. beneficiaries) will use that money, putting it into a trust will give you control over how it is used, even after you die.

Here's how it works: Instead of giving the money to a beneficiary straight out, a trust sets up a fund with a guardian, called a trustee. Only the trustee can access the funds, and the trustee is only allowed to use those funds to help the beneficiary according to specific instructions that YOU write when the trust is created. This protects your money and makes sure it's used the way you want it to be used.

Also, a will can only have power over assets after a person's death while a trust can come into effect in case you are incapacitated and could be used to provide funds for your care while you are still alive.

Gifting assets into a trust is a good way to protect them from federal estate taxes and leaves more money for your beneficiaries. Better yet, creditors who may be hounding your children for money can't seize assets placed in a trust.

A will has to go through the courts and probate fees before it can go into effect, but trusts don't have to do that. Using a trust to avoid probate equals BIG financial savings. In California an estate worth $500,000 (the average cost of a modest home) requires probate fees of $26,000 or more when a judge has to approve the distribution of assets.

Emergency Guardians for Minors Authorization

This is a HUGE hole in most parent's estate plans. They name guardians for minor children in their will, but since a will only comes into effect after death, it makes no provision for temporary guardianship in case the parents are injured or incapacitated.

Here's what we mean:

Sarah and Ben were seriously injured in a car accident on the way home from dinner. Both are in comas and when the police go to the house to contact the family, they find a 16-year-old babysitter at home with two minor children.

The children are taken into protective custody, which means foster care.

The children remain in foster care until a judge can appoint temporary guardians. Though Sarah and Ben named their friends, Mike and Jane, as temporary guardians in their will, a will is not effective while they are still alive and has no bearing on where the children are placed if one of the parents is still alive.

To avoid having your children placed into foster care, fill out an Emergency Guardian for Minors Authorization form and make it available to babysitters and those named to care for your children in case of an emergency.

Health Care Power of Attorney

If you are incapacitated and unable to make health care decisions for yourself, a Health Care Power of Attorney will allow someone you trust to make those decisions for you, instead of leaving those decisions to the state.

Even your 18-year-old college student needs his or her own Health Care Power of Attorney. Without it, you won't have authority to make health care decisions for your child if they are injured or fall ill.

Living Will

A living will explains your wishes for life prolonging medical treatments such as life support and mechanical respiration.

This is a conversation we started with the Terri Shivago example. If you don't want to be kept alive with medical heroics such as life support and artificial feeding tubes, then you MUST sign and make available a living will that documents your decisions about life support. It is only effective if you are in an irreversible coma or a persistent vegetative state.

Advance Medical Directive

Living wills are often combined with Health Care Power of Attorney to create a document called the Advance Medical Directive. With these documents, you are making medical decisions for the future.

Third Party HIPAA Release

This document gives permission for someone you trust to access private medical information.

During the Virginia Tech shooting in 2007, thousands of phone calls flooded local hospitals as panicked parents tried to ascertain whether their college age children were wounded, dead, or alive and well.

Because of federal privacy laws, hospital personnel were forbidden to answer those questions. Why? Because those same students hadn't filled out the necessary forms that would allow medical personnel to discuss their medical condition with their parents. There were no HIPAA releases.

When naming people to be your health care agents in case of incapacitation, make sure they are also named on an HIPAA release. This assures that they'll be able to communicate with medical professionals if tragedy strikes.

Organ Donation Authorization

Even though you may have marked "organ donor" on your driver's license, an Organ Donation Authorization form can specify exactly what organs you'd like to donate and for what reasons. If you want to donate your brain for scientific research, then this is the form that you need.

In addition to marking your driver's license to let emergency personnel know that you are an organ donor, we encourage you to talk to your family to avoid any confusion about what is to be done with your body.

General Durable Power of Attorney

When you give Power of Attorney to someone you trust, it means that if you become incapacitated, this person can sign your name and make decisions on your behalf for the financial assets and property in your name.

If a family member, we'll call him Bob, had a traumatic brain injury and is no longer able to make decisions on his own, a Power of Attorney would make it easy for his wife, Helen, to handle his financial affairs. But if there is no Power of Attorney, then follows a lengthy process where the courts will determine if Bob is mentally incompetent. Imagine Helen's heartache as she watches Bob go through psychic evaluations while she herself is interviewed to find out exactly how incompetent her husband has become. This process is lengthy, painful, and humiliating for everyone involved. But if someone has Power of Attorney, there's no need for it.

It's also wise to give someone Power of Attorney if you are traveling abroad, in case something happens to you while you are in a different country.

A Note About Medical Documents

We recommend that you store a copy of your medical documents with a company like Legal Vault, Docubank or Legal Directive. These companies store an electronic copy on their database and send you an Emergency Access card to put in your wallet. Doctors and hospitals use this card to access your medical documents via fax or the Internet so that they immediately know who has access to your medical information and who to contact in case medical decisions need to be made. It's a lot easier than hauling around a file full of papers in your wallet in case of a medical emergency.

Worksheet 1:
The Checklist

Here's a quick summary of all the basic estate planning documents. When you call a lawyer to design an estate-planning package, check off these items as he/she lists what is available. If anything is missing, ask him if it can be added.

- ❑ **Will**—instructions for distributing your financial assets and personal property.
- ❑ **Trust**—Appoints a trustee to manage financial assets for your beneficiaries so that those funds will not be misused.
- ❑ **Emergency and Permanent Guardians for Minors Nomination**—Authorizes temporary guardians for your children in case of injury or illness and prevents them from staying in a foster home.
- ❑ **Advance Health Care Directive**—In California, this is a single document that includes a Living Will and Health Care Power of Attorney.
- ❑ **Health Care Power of Attorney**—Empowers someone you trust to make health decisions for you if you can't make them yourself.
- ❑ **Living Will**—Expresses your wishes about being put on life support.
- ❑ **Third Party HIPAA Release**—Gives permission for health care personnel to disclose details about your medical condition to a third party.
- ❑ **Organ Donation Authorization**—Certifies your decision to be an organ donor, and you can authorize the donation of your organs for scientific research.
- ❑ **General Durable Power of Attorney**—Appoints someone you trust to handle your financial affairs if you become incapacitated or die unexpectedly.

Worksheet 2:
Persons to Act For You

This worksheet helps you start a list of trusted people that can help you with your estate plan. The same person can be chosen for more than one role, but each role has different responsibilities.

Be sure to name backups in case your primary choice is unable or unwilling to serve at the time. You don't know when someone will move away, suffer an illness or injury, or go through a divorce that changes his or her ability to help you.

Because each situation is different, consider talking with the people on your list (even your backups) and ask them if they are willing to serve. They may need fair warning if tragedy strikes.

Guardians for Minor Children
(Both emergency and permanent)

Here you'll list two groups of people below—those you approve to be guardians for your children, and those you want to avoid. The second group is your list of "undesirables," meaning they're so unfit to be guardians that foster care is the better alternative.

Here are some questions to consider before you make your choice:

1. Where does the potential guardian live? Children move to where the guardian is, not the other way around
2. What are the religious, political, and moral beliefs of the potential guardian?
3. What do you know about the potential guardian's parenting skills?

4. How old is the potential guardian? Do they have the time and the strength to raise your children?
5. What is the potential guardian's family situation? Are they single, married with no children, married with young children, married with older children, or do they have a blended family?
6. What is the potential guardian's financial situation? Are they good with managing money? Do they have a stable job?
7. Who could be a backup in case something happens to the guardians you name?

Name and Address for APPROVED guardians:
Relationship

____

____

____

____

____

____

____

Name and Address for UNAPPROVED Guardians:
Relationship

____

____

____

____

____

____

____

Trust Guardian Nomination:

If you choose to put some of your assets in a trust, who would be the best person to manage those assets and wisely distribute them to your beneficiaries?

Here are some questions to consider:

1. Does this person have the knowledge and experience to make wise investments?—it's not enough to be trustworthy. Whoever you pick needs to have the financial expertise necessary to handle the assets in the trust properly.
2. Is this person financially responsible?
3. Do you trust them to make the best decisions to benefit your heirs?
4. Who could be a backup in case something happens to them or they are unwilling to serve?
5. Would it be better to appoint a neutral third party instead of a family member?

Name and Address:

Relationship

____

____

____

____

____

____

____

____

Attorney in Fact:

This is the person who would have Power of Attorney over your financial affairs if you were unable to make decisions for yourself. You may have one or more people serving at the same time. Married couples often list their spouse as the first choice and have alternatives listed if their spouse is unable to serve.

Here are some questions to consider:

1. Is this person financially responsible?
2. Would you trust this person to handle your finances and legal decisions the way YOU would want? With your best interest in mind?
3. Do you trust this person?
4. Who could be a backup in case something happens to them or they are unwilling to serve?

Name and Address:

Relationship

___

___

___

___

___

___

___

___

___

___

___

Health Care Agents

This applies to the Health Care Power of Attorney. These people will make medical decisions for you rather than financial decisions. Just like Trustee or Power of Attorney, you can appoint more than one person and married couples usually list their spouse as their first choice.

Here are some questions to consider before you make your choice:

1. Are they assertive enough to make strong decisions on your behalf?
2. Do they live close to you?
3. Do they understand your health conditions?
4. Will they have power both over finances AND medical decisions?
5. And most importantly of all, do you have complete trust in this person?
6. Who could be a backup in case something happens to your first choice or they are unwilling to serve?

Name and Address:

Relationship

____

____

____

____

____

____

Because each situation is different, consider talking with the people on your list (even your backups) and ask them if they are willing to serve. They may need fair warning if tragedy strikes.

If you don't take time to avoid probate now, your heirs will spend the time and pay for it later.

Chapter 3: To Probate or Not to Probate? That is the Question

After you die, what happens to your assets? If you have a good estate plan, your assets will be automatically transferred to your successor trustees or a surviving spouse if you've set up a survivorship option. In this way, assets can be distributed quickly and painlessly.

But if none of these provisions are established, your assets will then go through a process called probate. Probate is when the state courts take over your affairs after you die. They appoint a representative who handles the complicated paperwork, makes sure that all of your debts and taxes are settled, and THEN the representative can distribute the assets to your beneficiaries after being paid a hefty fee for their efforts. In California, the fee for managing an estate worth $500,000 is $26,000.

One of the biggest goals of estate planning is to avoid probate. If the estate plan is set up properly beforehand, then there is no need for a person's assets to go through this costly, lengthy process in the state courts.

In some situations, a lawyer may recommend a "dry probate" where no assets are involved. This allows for a final, ironclad settlement with any creditors wanting compensation for unpaid debts. Dry probate is recommended for people in high-risk business ventures so that their beneficiaries don't have to deal with any financial lawsuits in the future.

When choosing a lawyer for your estate plan, make sure you quiz him closely on how he will avoid probate with your estate plan.

They say possession is nine tenths of the law, but even possession can't trump owning title. Title is everything.

Chapter 4: Owning Your Assets

Ever seen a tug of war between two toddlers over a favorite toy? They both insist that the toy belongs to them and the parents have to figure out who's right. When we become adults we have titles and deeds that prove ownership, but when you die, these issues get complicated if you don't own your assets properly.

Here's an example:

Rodney remarried after his wife's death. He and Brenda, his second wife, put all their assets in joint names to reduce their taxes as they had both done in their first marriages. They did this with Rodney's house, bank accounts, and investment accounts. He even put Brenda's name on his retirement accounts and life insurance. Brenda did the same with her assets.

In their wills, they said that all their assets would go to their respective children from previous relationships.

Then, Rodney died in a car accident.
Rodney's will left everything he owned to his children.
What did Rodney's children inherit?
Nothing.
Why?

Rodney owned NOTHING in his individual name. The house, bank account, investment accounts—they all passed to the joint owner, Brenda.

Even Rodney's personal possessions passed to Brenda as they were deemed to be joint property.

Rodney's will can only control assets that are in his individual name. Since all of his assets had Brenda's name on them, his will has no power to pass on his assets to his children.

Will Brenda give any assets to Rodney's children?
No, she won't;

Rodney's children have been unintentionally disinherited because Rodney's estate plan did not match with how he owned his assets.

To avoid Rodney's situation, the first step is to find out how you own your assets—then you'll know what will happen to those assets upon your death. If your current ownership doesn't match up with the instructions you put in your estate plan, then you must change the title on those assets.

Revocable Living Trust

If you want your trust to control your assets then your assets must be titled in the name of your trust, not your individual name. For example, instead of Rodney putting his name on the title of his house, he should have put it in the name of the "Rodney Smith Living Trust dated December 12, 2013."

If you want your life insurance, bank accounts, brokerage accounts, mutual funds, or annuities to be controlled by your trust, then you must name your **TRUST** as the beneficiary, NOT your estate OR an individual.

Will

If you want your will to control your assets, you either must own those assets in your individual name or, for contract assets (life insurance, annuities, and retirement accounts), name your estate as the beneficiary.

To own your assets properly, this is what you do:

For trusts to control your assets, you need to put the title in the name of your trust and name the trust as the beneficiary for contract assets. Here's an example:

If you want your will to control your assets, make sure your individual name is on the title.

To emphasize – we're jumping up and down and yelling now – YOUR ESTATE PLAN WILL ONLY WORK IF YOU OWN YOUR ASSETS PROPERLY—if you don't, then your estate plan is a pile of useless papers.

Cash now, cash with strings, or cash later? It's up to you.

Chapter 5: Passing the Buck—Distributing Financial Assets

The bottom line for financial distribution is who gets what, how, and when.

Here are a few thoughts to consider:

- Who are your beneficiaries of specific dollar amounts or percentages of your estate?
- Who are beneficiaries of the residual interest – any assets not distributed by a specific gift?
- Will the inheritances be provided outright or in a trust?

We recommend working through a trust, unless the gift is small and going to be spent immediately. That being said, it may be wise to include even a small gift in a trust just in case the beneficiary is in the middle of a divorce or lawsuit when the inheritance becomes available. The trustee can end the trust before it even gets started if there is no need for asset protection.

Ask your attorney about the best way to distribute your assets.

- Who will serve as trustees of the beneficiary trusts?

  Remember to never let a beneficiary serve as the sole trustee of their share of the trust. If you do, it can be taken from them through a lawsuit or divorce.
- What happens if your beneficiary dies before you do?

It's common to give the assets that would have gone to the beneficiary to the beneficiary's children or to the other beneficiaries named in the trust.

- What happens if your beneficiary dies with assets still in his or her trust?

You can let the beneficiary decide, or they would go to whom you name—typically siblings, children, or grandchildren.

Prepare for the storm, even if you think it will never come.

Chapter 6: Incapacity Planning

You are six times more likely to become incapacitated through illness or injury this year than it is likely for you to die. Incapacity planning is essential to an estate plan that works. It keeps you in control and avoids court interference if you become too ill or injured to manage your everyday finances and decisions.

Documents

Here's a list of estate planning documents that are involved with incapacity planning:

1. Power of Attorney
2. Revocable Living Trust
3. Medical forms
    a. Health Care Power of Attorney
    b. HIPAA release

Decisions

In the documents listed above, you'll be able to make the following decisions:

1. Who will determine whether you are incapacitated and how will that determination be made?

    The definition of incapacitation is generally understood as: "When the Trustmaker is unable to effectively manage his or her property or financial affairs because of age, illness, mental disorder, dependence on prescription medication or other substances, or any other cause."

Basically, if you are unable to make day-to-day decisions and you are unable to manage your assets, then you are considered incapacitated.

Many folks appoint a disability panel consisting of loved ones and medical doctors to determine whether they are incapacitated or not. These people would be the Health Care Agents you listed in chapter two.

2. How do I want to live my life if I am incapacitated?

In your estate plan you can decide how your money will be used to care for you if you are incapacitated. You can do this by setting up a Revocable Living Trust and set aside assets to fund your care. For example, individuals who want to avoid a nursing home make provisions for home care and leave instructions if they still want to participate in their favorite activities like visiting the park or attending sporting events.

Individuals who are married or in a committed relationship usually indicate their assets can be used to care for themselves and their significant other. If they have minor children and pets, they can leave instructions that their funds should be used to care for children and pets as well.

3. Who will care for my children and pets?

If you are alive, but unable to care for your children (mentally or physically), then the temporary guardians you listed in chapter two will step in to support you and those you love. In chapter seven there is a worksheet where you can list caretakers for your pets and find more details on pet planning.

To see unconditional love, observe the bond between a pet and its owner.

Chapter 7: Pet Planning

Pets are often forgotten in estate planning and as a result, many pets are turned out into the street after their owners die. Here's your chance to name people who would be willing to take care of your pets when you are unable to do so yourself. These people would be named in your will as pet caretakers.

If you'd like to leave instructions for your pet's trust as to living arrangements, daily care, and medical care, you are free to do that as well. You can also put aside some money in a trust to help pay for the care of your pets if you are capable of doing so. If you include a trust for your pets in the estate plan, you will also need to name a trustee for those funds. Often, the pet caretaker and the trustee are the same person.

Here are some questions to consider as you make your choice for a pet caretaker and/or a trustee:

1. Do they like animals?
2. Would they have enough room to house your pets?
3. Do they have the financial means to care for your pets?
4. Who could be a backup in case something happens to the first guardians you name?

List four possible candidates for pet caretakers below:

Name and Address: Relationship

____

____

____

____

Etch your name in the lives of others, and the stories they share about you will be a legacy that touches lives for generations.

Chapter 8: Your Legacy

Aside from financial assets, what else will you leave behind? How do you want to be remembered? Estate Planning is not just for distributing your financial assets. Estate Planning can also help you leave a legacy for your posterity.

There is so much that your children, grandchildren, and other loved ones don't know about you and your life. This incredibly valuable information is part of your legacy and should be shared with the people you love the most.

Dr. Barrie Sanford Greiff of Harvard Medical School wrote:

Many people I meet and talk with every day openly question whether we have become too "caught up in the thick of thin things"…I sense a yearning in these people, a desire to pass on something more than the material wealth they have accumulated. They want to pass on something of themselves – something of the spirit – of who they are and what they have meant…many seem to say, "My life has more relevance than simple economics after a lifetime of living and contribution. I refuse to be thought of as a balance sheet."

The purpose of this chapter is to provide tools and examples of how others have preserved their own legacies. There is no one way to record a legacy. Look over the tools described here and decide which method would be the best one for you. Use the worksheets at the end of the chapter to help you get started. Feel free to pick and choose the methods you like and make it your own. We also advise that you don't wait—share your legacy with your family while you're alive and well.

Create Your Book of Life

The first and most common method of creating a legacy is to make a personal book of life where you document the highlights of your life.

Grab a notebook or a bunch of index cards of any size and color. Some like to use the cards that are connected on a ring, but a rubber band or a hair band works just as well to keep your cards together.

Mark each card to represent one year on your life. So, if you're 30, you'll have 30 cards, numbered 1 through 30; if you're 54, you'll have 54 cards, numbered 1 through 54.

Jot down something for each year, including highlights, events, thoughts, people who influenced you, or a list of your closest friends.

When your index cards are finished, transfer that information into a book that can be given to your family and friends.

We suggest that you keep your cards around, perhaps in the drawer next to your bed, so you can add to them when a new memory or observation surfaces.

Even if the information you gather never gets into a book, the stack of index cards will still be a valuable legacy for your family that we encourage you to share. Use the cards to tell your family what you've remembered or use your Book of Life to formally document your legacy.

Personal Messages

When you are no longer around to express yourself, the most treasured possession you can leave behind is documentation – physical proof – of your love for your friends and family. One way to do this is through personal messages. These messages can be written, videotaped, or even voice recorded. With today's technology, recording videos can even be done with webcams and cell phones.

Before you record your messages, make a list of who should receive them: your children, your closest friends, your spouse, or a mentor. In your message, explain to this person how you feel about them and why they are important to you. Share stories about things this person did or said that made you happy. How did they influence your life for the better?

Record Family Stories

The New York Times article "The Stories That Bind Us" reveals that one of the most important ingredients for a happy, resilient family is a family narrative—stories about the good times, the hard times, and how the family stuck together through it all.

When you're at a family reunion, the best part is when you are listening to stories fly back and forth among relatives. These stories are a valuable part of your history. While spending time with family, record these stories on audio and/or video. You can use your Book of Life cards to stimulate stories at family gatherings and record them as you go.

The stories that you record will be a gift to your loved ones that they can treasure for the rest of their lives. Take this opportunity to make sure your family stories will make it to the next generation.

Sentimental Gifts

Another way to preserve a legacy is to choose a special gift of sentimental value for each of your loved ones. Monetary gifts are appreciated, but sentimental gifts are truly treasured.

There are no rules for gifts other than to be sure the gifts are of similar financial value and if you include one person in a class, include them all. For example, if you provide a sentimental gift for one grandchild, leave a similar gift for each of your grandchildren.

Here are examples:

- Elsie and her granddaughter, Katie, played tea party when Katie was a little girl. Elsie made sure that Katie would receive that tea set when she passed.
- Ben always read The Big Red Barn and The Night Before Christmas to his son, Jake. When Jake's first child was born, Ben passed along the treasured books to him to read to his own son.
- Michael rang the dinner bell each and every Sunday at his grandparents' home. So, in their estate plan, his grandparents made sure that Michael would receive that same dinner bell after they died.

Many jot down a list and keep it with their important papers. Your list might say something like "My engagement ring to my grandson, Matthew, for him to present to the love of his life, since his grandfather was the love of my life."

Make sure your estate plan very clearly states who gets what gift—the purpose of sentimental gifts is to express love and preserve memories, not to inspire confusion or contention.

Ethical Will

If you want to focus your legacy on the lessons you've learned throughout your life, you can do this with something called an "Ethical Will."

In your Ethical Will, you jot down what you've learned in your life and any message and guidance you'd like to pass along based on those life lessons. An Ethical Will passes on your wisdom to future generations.

Here are some examples:

- Barb wanted to be sure that if something happened to her, the guardians she named would teach her children as she would. To accomplish this, Barb wrote down her Top 10 Life Lessons I Share with My Children.

- Sam and Amanda went through many financial difficulties during their marriage, so they created a list of guiding principles to be presented by their trustees to their beneficiaries before any monies could be distributed from their trust.
- Suzanne and Neil greatly believed in community service, so they left a letter showing how they had contributed to their town as well as the benefits both the family and the community reaped. They encouraged their children and grandchildren to do the same.

If you're having trouble thinking of what to put in your ethical will, consider this question: "If I only had fifteen minutes left to speak with my children, what would I say?"

Financial Legacies

Financial legacies combine monetary assets with the goals of your estate plan. Here are some examples:

- Set up a college fund for your grandchildren or children.
- Donate books to the library in honor of those you love and admire.
- Sponsor a tree or bench in the park.
- Pay for a cage for a dog or cat at your local animal shelter.
- Set up a charitable trust or a private foundation.

There is no right or wrong when it comes to leaving a legacy.

Worksheet 3
Who Am I?

Documenting an entire life seems intimidating at first, but these worksheets will help you narrow your focus and record the things that are of the most value. Let's get started by using a legacy tool I learned from Scott Farnsworth, President of Sunbridge, Inc. and Founder of the Legacy Builder Network. For this activity, you complete the following three sentences:

1. My name is ________________, I live in ________________, and I (add a personal detail about yourself) ____.
2. I come from a people who were:

_________________, _________________, And ________________.

3. From these people I learned:

_________________, _________________, And ________________.

This exercise can be as short as three sentences or as long as three pages. Here's what I wrote after trying this exercise myself:

My name is E. Lawrence Brock and I live in Chino Hills, California. Almost anyone I meet, I consider a friend.

I come from a people who were hard working, the salt of the earth, extremely patriotic, dedicated, and committed to our country. My father was from the big city, growing up in Los Angeles. He was a second-generation Angelino. My mother was from a very small town in northeast Utah. Her father homesteaded in that community and established a farm around 1912. My parents came from very different backgrounds, which gave me full exposure to different life lessons and experiences, but with a common belief system and a united focus. This influenced all the important lessons I learned from my parents.

From them, I learned the importance of family, the support that comes from family and friends, and to work hard. If you wanted something you had to work for it; if you worked for it, you would receive rewards and satisfaction. I was taught that achievements in life are obtained by participating, working, and serving others. My parents taught me deep and abiding faith, along with confidence in myself and my ability to complete the job that I had undertaken.

This exercise gives you a quick summary of yourself and can help you decide what else should be included in your legacy.

Worksheet 4:
What Really Matters

On the next two pages, use the charts to help you figure out which values are important to you. I believe that as you identify treasured values and share why those values are important to you, it will become a positive influence on your life and the lives of your children. Including your most important values in your estate plan creates a family a document that becomes a glue to hold your family together for the future.

Honor
Love
Responsibility
Faith
Leadership
Philanthropy & Service
Forgiveness
Compassion
Integrity
Honesty
Choices & Accountability
Success
Hope
Work
Patience
Loyalty

Friendly
Courteous
Reverent
Relationships
Commmitment
Faithfulness
Gratitude
Knowledge
Wisdom
Family Unity
Good Health & Attitude
Refreshment/Replenishment
Humiliy
Sacrifice
Virtue
Respect

Worksheet 4 Continued

After you've identified your top three values, the next step is to record the following:

1. What do my values mean to me?

Value 1: ______________________

Definition:____

Value 2: ______________________

Definition:____

Value 3: ______________________

Definition:____

2. Write down the stories of how and when these values became important to you:

Value 1

____

____

____

____

Value 2

____

____

____

____

Value 3

____

3. Last of all, what do you want your children to learn from these values?

A priest, a doctor, and a lawyer went to a funeral...

Chapter 9: Funeral Arrangements

It may surprise you to know, but funeral, burial, memorial service, or life celebration arrangements, along with personal property, cause the most family discord among all estate planning issues.

When tragedy strikes, emotions run high and old hurts and resentments often come to the surface. The more decisions you can make ahead of time, the better.

It doesn't matter if you want a traditional funeral or a party on the beach, just make sure you write it down and let family members know your wishes. The more specific you make your instructions, the better. Make sure this information is kept with the rest of your estate planning documents in a place where your family can access it. It won't do any good to create a plan if no one can find it.

Worksheet 5:
Funeral Arrangements

What is my religious membership or spiritual beliefs?

____

____

____

I desire that services be: ❑ for friends and relatives or ❑ private

Desired location for the funeral:

____

____

____

____

Describe the type of funeral you would like to have:

____

____

____

____

Clergy:

____

____

Pallbearers:

____

____

____

____

Scripture Selections:

Music selections:

Other Readings:

Viewing Wishes: ❑ open casket ❑ closed casket

Notes:

For want of a signature, an estate plan failed and the litigation continued for seven years. Use this chapter to make sure your heirs aren't stuck in court for a decade.

Chapter 10: What Do You Mean My Estate Plan Might Fail?

The best hot pastrami sandwich in the country is on the corner of 7th Street and Alvarado in downtown Los Angeles at Langer's Deli. The delicious, chewy bread combined with their mouthwatering pastrami makes a sandwich that's worth dying for. But this wonderful restaurant is just fifty feet away from a dangerous area of LA—MacArthur Park. Turn right, and you'll get a top-rated pastrami sandwich. But if you turn left, you could be mugged or worse.

Estate plans are just like getting a sandwich on 7th and Alvarado. If you do your estate plan exactly right, then you get a top-rated pastrami sandwich—an estate plan that does exactly what you want. But if one sentence is out of place, the whole thing could be ruined and you'll be trekking through MacArthur Park, surrounded by thieves ready to tear you apart.

The Top 9 Reasons Estate Plans Fail

Online Forms:

In the past 10 years, online document businesses have become a cheaper, more attractive option for creating estate plans. You type in your information on a website and a few days later, a nicely packaged will shows up in the mail, ready to be signed and witnessed. The process is sold as quick, painless, and easy…until a judge has to sit down and interpret it.

Unfortunately, estate plans often fail when they are created through Do-It-Yourself (DIY) legal services rather than through certified lawyers. DIY legal services like LegalZoom and Rocket Lawyer can churn out legal documents very quickly, but their services are cheap because qualified attorneys do not draft your documents. Instead, employees called 'processors' add your information to a set of standard forms. These employees are not legal professionals. They are not trained to see potential weaknesses in your estate plan. They are NOT lawyers.

When you create an estate plan with a lawyer, he legally represents you and is responsible for any inconsistencies in the documents. If any problems arise because of how he prepared the document, he is liable for damages and can be sued for malpractice.

But if you use a DIY legal service, YOU are responsible. Here's part of LegalZoom's disclaimer from 2013: "LegalZoom is not a law firm, and the employees of LegalZoom are not acting as your attorney. LegalZoom's legal document service is not a substitute for the advice of an attorney." If there are any mistakes in your documents or your estate plan doesn't do what it was supposed to, the DIY service is not responsible—YOU are responsible as if you were your own lawyer. Unfortunately, you can't sue yourself for malpractice. Although DIY legal services are cheaper, they come with a heavy price.

I've seen horrid cases of children unintentionally disinherited, living trusts that aren't honored by financial institutions, documents improperly executed and therefore invalid, children with drug problems having immediate access to funds that fueled their addictions, and family fights ending in litigation because language was unclear on a DIY estate plan.

Time and time again, estate planning lawyers are hired to clean up the mess that DIY services create – this costs the clients far more than if they had received sound legal advice in the first place. And even though some DIY businesses offer a consulting service with professional lawyers, the people you talk to are NOT authorized to act as your legal representative. Technically, you are still representing yourself.

If you want your estate plan done right, pay the money to get it drafted by a qualified attorney. At the website www.estateplandesigner.com, your information is sent to a lawyer in your state who drafts a custom estate plan that perfectly fits your needs. This lawyer is designated as your legal representative and if he makes a mistake, he is responsible for the damages, not you.

The reason it's important to have a professional lawyer draft your estate plan is because no matter your situation in life, a professional can make sure that your estate plan addresses potential problems with clear language that will stand up in court.

Estate Planning Documents Not Available

Another way your estate plan can fail is if your loved ones can't find your documents. If this happens, all efforts to avoid probate will be ruined. The state will step in and decide what happens—meaning you won't get to decide who inherits from you, who helps you, or who raises your children.

To ensure that your estate planning documents are available, tell your loved ones where you keep them: it could be in a filing cabinet or on the shelf in your home office. If you want to keep it in a safe or safety deposit box, just make sure someone besides you has the key or combination so it can be opened. If you keep it in a filing cabinet, place the documents in the middle drawer so they'll be safe from flood or fire.

Some people put their estate plan into a safety deposit box. But the laws regarding access to safety deposit boxes after death vary from state to state, so find out more information before you decide to put your will in the bank. In California, a lawyer is allowed to look in the safety deposit box for a will, but in other states, he is not.

Documents are Not Up-to-Date

Life can take unexpected turns, so it's a good idea to update your estate plan every five years. You also need to update your estate plan every time you move to a new state, get married, get divorced, enter into a committed relationship, end a committed relationship, have or adopt a child, start a business, or have a significant change in assets.

If you remarry and your estate plan has not been updated, your children could be accidentally disinherited because your spouse may receive your assets instead of your children.

Wishes of the Deceased Are Unclear

If your loved ones interpret the instructions on your estate plan in different ways, their opinions could turn into fights that would tear the family apart.

If you want your estate plan to work, the instructions must be crystal clear. A qualified attorney can make sure there is no confusion in your documents.

Make sure that specific instructions concerning your burial and funeral arrangements are also included in your estate plan (see worksheet #5 in Chapter 9). There can be just as many fights over burial arrangements as there could be about the inheritance.

No Instructions Are Given for Distributing Personal Items

It may surprise you to know this, but most family battles over inheritances aren't about the money. Why? Because money can easily be divided into 2, 3, 4, or even 20 shares.

On the other hand, personal property with sentimental value can't be evenly divided in halves, thirds, or fourths, etc.

If you take our advice and use sentimental gifts to leave a legacy, you can present gifts to your loved ones during your lifetime or include a memorandum that explains who receives which gifts, and attach it to a will or trust.

If you think that a gift could be controversial, include specific instructions and an explanation about that gift in your memorandum. Any gifts mentioned in a memorandum are legally enforceable.

Blended Families

Blended families, remarriages, divorces, and step-children make estate planning more complicated. When you make an estate plan, make sure your attorney fully understands your family situation so that no one is accidentally disinherited.

Traumatic Events

When your children become adults, they can be subject to bad divorces, lawsuits, medical difficulties, addictions, failing businesses, or massive debts.

If you give everything to your children outright in a will, all of those assets can be taken away from them with one lawsuit. But with a well-designed trust, creditors can't touch them.

Life happens, but you can avoid throwing your children's inheritance out the window if you use trusts to protect your assets after you die.

Pets Aren't Protected

Pets are often overlooked in estate plans. If there are no instructions about pets in an estate plan, those pets are often let out the back door to fend for themselves or they're dropped off at a shelter. You need to name a caretaker for your pet and a trustee to handle money that pays to feed and house your pet.

Assets Aren't Owned Properly

If the titles of your assets aren't in alignment with your estate plan, it will fail. If you have a trust, make sure your assets are titled in the name of that trust. If you are depending on a will to distribute your assets, make sure they are in your own, individual name, not in joint ownership with your spouse.

Most couples choose joint ownership for their assets because it's a quick and easy way to do estate planning. When one spouse dies, the other spouse inherits everything outright and automatically—no probate, no fees, no fuss. But this system only works for traditional, nuclear families with no divorces and no second marriages. Consider the following situations:

1. What if it's a second marriage and the parents want their assets to go to their own children?

2. What if the surviving spouse finds a new partner who convinces him/her to lend money to start a new business? This would drain the assets that should have gone to the children.

3. What if the surviving spouse is sued in malpractice, goes bankrupt, or gets divorced in a subsequent marriage? Again, all of your assets would be drained and nothing would be left for your children to inherit.

There is no benefit to joint ownership. Good estate plans use other methods to protect your assets.

Worksheet #6
Why Estate Plans Fail

While discussing your estate plan with your lawyer, go over this checklist to make sure that all potential problems with your estate plan have been considered.

1. Have I used ANY fill-in-the-blank legal forms from the Internet? If so, discard them immediately.
2. Have I put my estate planning documents in a safe place that is accessible to my family or trusted friends?
3. Have I updated my estate planning documents in the last five years?
4. Are my wishes stated in clear, undisputable language in my will?
5. Have I included clear instructions for my funeral arrangements?
6. Did I give instructions on how to distribute my personal items?
7. If I have a blended family, have I made provisions with my attorney to make sure that all the right people get their inheritance?
8. Have I put my assets in a trust to protect them from my children's creditors or other events like lawsuits and divorce?
9. Are all of my assets owned under the proper name?
10. Have I named a caretaker for my pets and left instructions for their care?

If all else fails, read the instructions.

Chapter 11: They Put Me in Charge, So What the Heck Do I Do Now?

This chapter is for you if you've been named as an agent, trustee, executor, or personal representative of someone's estate. Before we dive into the specific duties, here are the seven things you need to remember:

1. Always look to the document that authorizes you to act, whether it be a will, a trust, or a memorandum. This is where your loved one's wishes are documented. Make sure that what you are doing is fulfilling those wishes.
2. If you don't understand the documents pertaining to you, contact the attorney who drafted the document. The attorney will guide you through it and answer any questions you have.
3. Remember that you are always acting in the best interests of the beneficiary named in the document—NOT your own.
4. When you need help, and it's normal to need help, get it. This means that you should consult with the attorney, CPA, financial advisor, insurance professional, realtor, appraiser, or whatever professional is appropriate for your position. The trust or estate will pay for professional services, so don't worry about the cost.
5. NEVER EVER commingle funds by putting trust, estate, or beneficiary money in your personal bank account.
6. NEVER use trust, estate, or beneficiary funds for yourself, except as authorized in the document and approved by the attorney. But, it's okay to accept payment for your services.
7. Last of all, keep good records. Keep all receipts and write down expenses, bills, income, and decisions made while fulfilling the duties of your position.

Here's a list of trusted helpers and their duties:

Guardians for Minor Children:

Your job is to raise and care for the minor children entrusted to you on a daily basis. You will make health care, education, religious, lifestyle, and general welfare decisions on the children's behalf until they turn 18.

You'd normally think that guardians only have to serve if the client dies, but this isn't always true. If the right documents are in place, the guardians will also serve if the parents are incapacitated due to illness or injury and are still alive.

If you are named as an emergency guardian for the minors, then it is your job to watch over the children until the primary guardian arrives. You are the reason the children won't have to go into foster care while they wait for their permanent guardians.

Health Care Agents:

As the Health Care Agent, you are in charge of making decisions about the trust maker's medical care. You are not in charge of finances other than to authorize medical care that requires money.

You are the one who communicates with medical professionals like doctors and nurses and makes decisions for the trust maker. For example, you would decide if your client should undergo an operation or change medical providers.

As a health care agent, you should be strong and confident and willing to go head-to-head with a doctor to fight for the proper medical care. You may have to say "no" to a recommended procedure because you feel it violates the living will of your client. If the hospital staff is too busy to provide proper care, assertively ask for more care and/or hire a private caretaker.

Financial Power of Attorney Agents and Incapacity Trustees:

You are the one who handles financial issues. You must pay bills, organize finances, manage assets, take care of property, and make sure taxes are filed.

ALWAYS act in the best interests of your client. Invest conservatively and keep a record of all your transactions. NEVER commingle your funds with theirs. It is against the law to financially benefit from your client's assets unless there are specific instructions that allow it.

For example, if an estate plan authorizes a $10,000 gift to all grandchildren and you, the agent, are also a grandchild, you may accept the gift along with your siblings and cousins.

Executor and Settlement Trustees:

Executors and settlement trustees carry out the instructions in a will or trust for distributing assets. You must follow the instructions listed in the estate plan and those required by state and federal law.

Your main duties include gathering, inventorying, protecting, and managing assets. You also pay the final bills and file the last tax return. After the state or federal government has accepted the taxes, then assets can be distributed to the named beneficiaries.

If there is no will or trust, the court will appoint an administrator to take care of all of these matters.

Trustees of Beneficiary Trusts:

If you have been named as a trustee of a beneficiary trust, your main job is the follow the directions in the trust document. Look to the trust document for instructions on investment and management advice. File the tax returns and say "no" to any creditor who tries to seize the money.

ONLY use the assets in the trust according to the instructions, or you can be sued for damages.

In case you need help (which is very common), you can hire attorneys, CPAs, or financial advisors for guidance. In most cases, it is permissible use funds from the trust to hire professional help.

Pet Caretakers and Pet Trust Trustees:

Pet caretakers take care of the client's pets on a daily basis. Your job is to love, feed, groom, administer medicine and take the pet to a veterinarian.

If you are a trustee for assets set aside for the pets, then you pay their bills and manage the money. You'll also want to check on the pets to make sure they are healthy and happy.

Relax. Lawyers don't bite. Their job is to protect YOU, and ***ONLY YOU***

Chapter 12: How Do I Choose an Attorney?

After going through this book, your next step is to choose a qualified attorney to draft your estate plan. You can choose to meet with a lawyer in person, or take advantage of the www.estateplandesigner.com web site so that a qualified attorney can draft your individual estate plan without you ever having to leave your house.

One of the best ways to find a good attorney is through personal references. Talk to your friends and ask them for recommendations. Remember that attorneys specialize in different fields, so look for an attorney who specializes in estate planning.

If your friends don't have any recommendations, you can look for attorneys in your area using the following resources:

www.estateplandesigner.com
www.wealthcounsel.com
www.estateplanning.com
www.naepc.org

Most attorneys will give you a free consultation where you can get a feel for their personality. Aside from certificates and credentials, the most important quality for an attorney is trust. Do you feel comfortable with this attorney? Your attorney will be privy to very sensitive information, so make sure he/she is someone you feel good about talking to.

Here are some questions you can ask yourself before you make your choice:

1. Do I feel comfortable with this attorney?
2. Does he/she communicate well?
3. Does this attorney specialize in estate planning?

4. Is their office within easy driving distance of my house?
5. Have they ever settled an estate posthumously? It requires more experience to settle an estate and get the money to the beneficiaries than it does to draft the estate plan. Lawyers who have settled estates are extremely knowledgeable in their field and will be better estate planners.

Worksheet #7
Choosing a Lawyer

Recommendations:

Ask your friends and family for recommendations. Make a list include the name of the person who recommended each lawyer to you.

1. ______________________________ Recommended by: _____________
2. ______________________________ Recommended by: _____________
3. ______________________________ Recommended by: _____________
4. ______________________________ Recommended by: _____________
5. ______________________________ Recommended by: _____________

Internet Search:

Do an Internet search for lawyers in your area. Copy their name, phone number, and travel time from your house to his/her office.

1. ____________________________________ Phone#: _______________
   a. ____ miles away from my house
2. ____________________________________ Phone#: _______________
   a. ____ miles away from my house
3. ____________________________________ Phone#: _______________
   a. ____ miles away from my house
4. ____________________________________ Phone#: _______________
   a. ____ miles away from my house
5. ____________________________________ Phone#: _______________
   a. ____ miles away from my house

Contact the lawyers on your list and arrange to meet with them or talk with them over the phone

Chapter 13: How Do I Choose an Estate Plan Package?

Now it's time to talk prices. Estate plan packages come in many shapes and sizes—the one you choose depends on your situation and on how much you want to spend. Here's a quick summary of general price ranges for estate plans:

DIY and Bare Bones estate plans: $69-1,100
Middle Grade estate plans: $1,4000-5,000
Luxury Grade estate plans: $10,000+

Okay, don't hyperventilate. Yes, it's true that an estate plan worth your money will likely cost $2,000 or more. Fortunately, paying a mere $2,000 up front can mean huge savings in the future and financial security for your family.

Do-It-Yourself (DIY) legal businesses like LegalZoom are the cheapest. They can do a will for as low as $69! But...you get what you pay for. DIY legal businesses are turning into an unexpected cash cow for lawyers because we are the ones getting paid to fix all the problems created by those same businesses. It's best to hire a professional lawyer from the beginning and get it right the first time, even though the price tag is a bit higher.

The cost of your estate plan also depends on which package you choose. In my office, we have four different estate plan packages at two different price ranges: The lower price is for plans drafted through the website www.estateplandesigner.com with one phone or office appointment. The higher price is for multiple face to face office consultations:

Basic Will (online: $495, in office: $850)

This plan is the least expensive and the most basic. It's designed for those who are just starting out, do not own a home, and have very few assets. This is a good plan for young families or young single adults. It includes the following documents:

Advanced Health Care Directive

HIPAA release of information form

Durable Power of Attorney

Will

Probate Avoidance (online $995, in office $1,350)

This plan includes a simple trust that will avoid probate and distribute assets immediately, directly, and equally to the children. This plan is meant for someone who owns a house, but not much more than that. Probate is avoided, but this plan does not include any provisions to protect your children's inheritance from creditors or life events. Documents included in this plan:

- Advanced Health Care Directive
- HIPAA release of information form
- Durable Power of Attorney
- Probate Avoidance Trust
- Pour-Over Will

Lifetime Trust (online $1,495-$2,495, in office $1,500-3,550)

This is a comprehensive estate plan that provides for incapacity or disability, protects the surviving spouse from creditors, liability, and remarriage, while providing options to establish lifetime trusts for the beneficiaries to protect their assets from creditors, liability, medical challenges, and failed marriages. Documents included in this plan:

- Advanced Health Care Directive
- HIPAA release of medical information form
- Durable Power of Attorney
- Pour-Over Will
- Revocable Living Trust
- Optional items:
- Special Needs Trust
- Tax Planning
- Bankruptcy
- Remarriage
- Medi-Cal
- Incapacity Planning
- Liability Protection
- Failed Marriage Protection

Purposeful Family Leadership Plan (online $3,000+, in office 5,500)

This is a comprehensive estate plan that includes personalized instructions rather than the standard legal language. If you only had 15 minutes left to live, what would you say to your family? This package gives you that opportunity.

Options included with this plan:

- Trusts for your grandchildren
- Family lifetime trust documents
- A recording that preserves your story for succeeding generations and gives guidance to your beneficiaries and trustees based on your values
- Lifetime trusts for children with incentives, guidance, and protection from creditors, failed marriage, bankruptcy, and lawsuits

A qualified attorney can change all of your worries into peace of mind.

Chapter 14: How Do I Prepare to Meet With My Attorney?

Once you've chosen an attorney, the first thing you do is remember that your attorney is highly qualified and their job is to take care of you. No matter your concerns, you will not shock the attorney and he/she will not judge you. There's likely nothing you could say that an estate-planning attorney hasn't heard before. Meetings with your attorney are completely confidential and designed to keep you safe. Before you sit down for your meeting, gather the following:

First, have all your questions and concerns written on a list. Leave room to jot down the answers to your questions because you'll have a lot of information flying at you that will be hard to remember when the meeting is over.

Next, bring a list of decisions that you've already made—this would include the worksheets from this book. For example, list the names of your sister and her husband as guardians of your children, your brother as your health care agent, and your mom as your trustee and financial Power of Attorney agent.

It's common for the attorney to ask you for a list of assets, goals, and family and professional advisor contact information, so have this information ready for him/her.

Last of all, bring any current estate planning documents that you already have, along with deeds, life insurance policies, and financial statements.

Paperwork

When you get to the attorney's office, this is some of the paperwork you'll likely have to fill out. Depending on which office you go to, these forms will look different since every attorney customizes office forms to fit the needs of their practice.

Your attorney will always be happy to answer your questions about the paperwork, so never hesitate to ask.

Confidential Personal Information Form (CPIF) – Your attorney needs to know all about you and your health, family, finances, goals, and concerns. The time and effort you invest in your CPIF will pay off ten-fold in creating an estate plan that is a good fit. And if you've completed the worksheets in this book, you already have a head start.

Engagement Agreement –No attorney should represent you unless you hire him or her in writing. The goal of the engagement agreement is to list all the things your attorney will do for you, the things you need to know, and the actions you need to take.

Couples Disclosure – If you are married, in a domestic partnership, or come to your attorney as a couple, your attorney represents you as a couple and cannot hide information from or act against the best interests of either one of you. If you hire the attorney as a couple, you're in it together.

Process Map – Your attorney may give you a diagram or letter that maps out the estate planning process so you know exactly what happens and when it happens.

It's not over until the fat lady sings.

Chapter 15: Am I Done?

Your lawyer has drafted a beautiful estate plan, you've signed it in the presence of all the proper witnesses, so now you can heave a sigh of relief and relax, right?

The most essential thing to remember is that once you receive your estate planning documents, you're NOT done. Estate planning is a constant process.

Here's what you do next:

Sign Your Documents with Care:

If you are signing your estate planning documents at home instead of in your attorney's office, be sure that you follow the signing instructions to the letter. You MUST follow ALL the rules, including witness and notary instructions EXACTLY as presented.

If your estate plan is NOT signed correctly with the correct number of witnesses, then the whole thing is null and void.

Chat with Loved Ones:

Tell your loved ones that you have created an estate plan. Keep all your estate planning documents together and within easy access for your friends and family.

If your estate planning documents can't be found or no one knows that they exist, all your planning will be in vain. Your loved ones will have to proceed as if you had never done any planning at all. This means probate, court interference, a loss of control, and higher fees.

Place Documents in a Safe Place:

If you put your documents in a safe deposit box, check your state laws to see if attorneys are allowed access to the box after death. If you keep the documents in a fire safe at home, be sure that your loved ones know the combination. If you keep your documents in a filing cabinet, choose a middle drawer and place the documents in the center of that drawer. This method protects documents against fire and flood.

Chat with Trusted Helpers:

Before you list someone as a guardian for your children or a financial power of attorney, talk with them first. Be sure that loved ones know they are named as trusted helpers and that they are okay with serving in that position. Give them the contact info of your attorney in case they have any questions or need help.

Update Your Wishes:

If your family situation or life situation changes, you may need to update your personal wishes for:

1. Gifts of personal property
2. Love letters, scrapbooks, photo albums, video and audio recordings, and any other legacy assets that are important to you.
3. Instructions for guardians for minor children.
4. Instructions for pet caretakers.
5. Funeral, burial, memorial service, and/or celebration of life arrangements.

Follow Through on Funding and Asset Ownership:

Your estate plan will only work if you follow through by ensuring that you own each and every asset in accordance with your estate plan.

If you want your trust to control assets, those assets must be titled in the name of the trust or the trust must be named as the beneficiary of contract assets such as life insurance and retirement accounts.

If you want your will to control your property, you must own that property in your individual name, not jointly with anyone else.

When you open a new bank account or investment account, be sure it's titled in the name of your trust. Or, if you want your will to control the account, keep it in your individual name.

If you have any questions about titling, check in with your attorney to find out exactly how you should own your assets to best ensure your estate plan works.

Keep Your Estate Plan Up-to-Date:

Be sure to have your estate plan professionally reviewed every three to five years. Your plan may not need to be updated that often, but life always changes.

Five years from now, it's likely you will have different goals, a different family situation, and different assets. The laws concerning estate plans may also have changed.

If you move to a new state, start a business, purchase a home, experience a significant change in assets, get married, get divorced, get remarried, have a new child, or adopt a child, your plan needs to be updated. Check in with your estate-planning attorney as these events happen to determine whether updates would be beneficial.

For example, if a trusted helper falls out of favor, moves away, becomes ill, or dies, your plan may need to be updated. I had a client who planned to give her house and care of her beloved dogs to a trusted friend. But a few years later she came back to take her friend's name off the estate plan because their relationship had changed enough that her friend had stopped talking to her and my client didn't know why.

If you want your estate plan to work, it must reflect your individual family and its evolution through regular and frequent reviews and updates. Estate planning is truly a process; it is not a "once and done" thing.

Once you've done all that, you're done! Celebrate. (That's an order.)

Worksheet #9
Updating Your Estate Plan Checklist

Whenever you update your estate plan, go through this checklist to make sure you've covered everything.

- ❑ Does my family know where my estate documents are?
- ❑ Are my trusted helpers still able and willing to serve?
- ❑ Do I need to take anyone off my estate plan?
- ❑ Do I need to add anyone to my estate plan?
- ❑ Am I living in a different state where estate-planning laws might be different?
- ❑ Do I still own all my assets properly?
- ❑ Do I need to change the title on assets I've recently acquired?
- ❑ Have I changed my mind about personal wishes for sentimental gifts, caretakers, or funeral arrangements?

Chapter 16: Estate Planning For the Internet Age

DIY legal businesses have become immensely popular because they provide the ultimate convenience—Have legal documents delivered to your doorstep without ever visiting an office.

But instead of using professional attorneys to draft their documents, DIY businesses use people without law degrees to churn out cookie cutter forms. It's convenient, but comes with its own risks and perils.

In this day and age, I've developed a new method of estate planning that combines the best of both worlds. The Estate Plan Designer website (www.estateplandesigner.com) connects clients with certified attorneys through the Internet. Your Certified Online Estate Planning Attorney is your attorney. He/she represents you, has legal duty to you, is licensed in your state, is experienced, will answer your questions and provide legal advice. Together you can avoid all the wrong turns and have the best estate plan possible.

Here's how it works:

Step 1: Complete the online educational and design interview.

On the website you will fill out a simple questionnaire—much of the same information given to you in this book. This gives attorneys the information they need to draft a custom estate plan to fit your needs.

Step 2: Review your information with one of our Certified Online Estate Planning Attorneys. This can be done over the phone or in person.

Your Certified Online Estate Planning Attorney is your attorney. He/she represents you, has legal duty to you, is licensed in your state, is experienced, will answer your questions and provide legal advice. Together you can avoid all the wrong turns and have the best estate plan possible.

If sometime in the future tragedy strikes and your trusted helpers need advice, your loved ones can call your Certified Online Estate Planning Attorney and get the help they need.

Step 3: Print your documents and sign them EXACTLY as instructed before witnesses and a notary.

That's it. It's easy.

By using the Estate Plan Designer program, you'll know the legal fee for your plan before you make any commitment. This process has no hidden fees and no unhappy surprises.

The only thing left to do is to keep your estate plan updated as the years go by.

Congratulations! You're finished!

I admire you.

I admire you because by reading this book you are taking action to create a legacy that will protect you and your family.

While most individuals understand they need have an estate plan, It's estimated that up to 63% of US citizens do not have one.

That means if tragedy strikes, millions and millions of individuals won't have the power to decide who raises their children, who makes their health care decisions, who manages their money, or who inherits their financial accounts and personal property.

But since you are reading this book, you are taking steps to protect the people you care about.

Best Wishes,
Larry Brock

Easy-to-Understand Estate Planning Glossary

Before we dive into definitions, let's clear up any confusion you may have on the labels we give to those who create an estate plan, those who carry out estate plan instructions, and those who benefit from an estate plan. Those labels change based on which estate planning document is used.

Creator:

- The creator of a trust is called a trust maker, trustor, or grantor.
- The creator of a will is called the testator if he is a male and a testatrix if she is a female.
- The person who creates a power of attorney document is the principal.

Manager:

- The person in charge of carrying out instructions in a trust is a trustee.
- If the document is a will, the person in charge of carrying out instructions is an executor if male, or executrix if female.
- If there was no will, the person appointed by the court to be in charge is the personal administrator.
- The person entrusted with power of attorney is the agent.

Spender:

- The person who benefits from an estate plan is called a "beneficiary."

Glossary

Administrator/Administratix: The person appointed by a court to administer and settle the estate of a person who dies without a will.

Administration Settlement Trustee: A trustee who gathers and attributes a value to all of the assets, reviews all debts, pays the appropriate debts, and distributes funds according to the terms of the trust.

Basis of Property: The baseline, monetary value used to determine gain or loss on sale of an asset. The basis is usually the cost of the property and this amount is used to calculate income taxes upon the sale of the asset.

Beneficiary: Any person who receives gifts/money/property from a will, trust, or life insurance policy.

Bequest: Money or property granted to a person (or an organization) in a will.

Bond: A guarantee by an insurance company agreeing to make up for any loss caused by an executor, administrator, or trustee through negligence or criminal activity.

Codicil: An amendment to a will. The requirements to make a codicil are the same as those for making a will. If you wish to make extensive changes, draft a new will rather than change the old one.

Community Property: Property acquired during the course of a marriage from the earnings or efforts of either spouse, except for property received by inheritance or gift. Community Property is recognized in eight states at the time of this writing: Arizona, California, Idaho, Louisiana, Nevada, New Mexico, Texas and Washington.

Conservatorship: A process in probate court that appoints a person to assume control over an individual's assets because that individual is deemed legally incompetent due to physical or mental incapacity. The use of a Revocable Living Trust can avoid a court appointed conservatorship by providing for the management of assets in case of legal incompetence or incapacity ahead of time.

Contingent Beneficiary: The beneficiary of a trust or will who receives trust assets or income after the death of the primary beneficiary. For example, if an heir dies before the trust maker, then the heir's children would inherit the estate.

Corpus (or Principal) of a Trust: The assets of a trust and their proceeds, separate from the income earned by the trust.

Decedent: A person who has died.

Devise, Legacy, Bequest: Legal terms used to mean property passed on through a will. Historically, devise refers to a gift of real estate, legacy refers to a gift of cash, and a bequest refers to a gift of personal property. Today, these terms are used interchangeably.

Distributive Share: The share of property inherited by a beneficiary after a decedent has died without a will. For example, when a person dies without a will and has no spouse and is survived by only one child, in most states the child inherits the entire estate. This would be the child's distributive share.

Durable Power of Attorney for Health Care (DPAHC): A special type of power of attorney that gives your agent the power to make certain types of health care decisions for you if you are unable to do so yourself because of your legal incompetence. See "Power of Attorney."

Equivalent Exemption (also known as Federal Equivalent Exemption): The amount of property that will pass on free of estate tax. This amount is currently $5,340,000.

Executor/Executrix: An individual or institution appointed to administer the estate of a deceased person. The executor legally steps into the shoes of the deceased and represents the estate in probate court. In some states, the executor is also called the personal representative.

Federal Estate Taxes: Taxes imposed on assets after the death of an individual. Federal estate taxes are determined by the size of the estate. The tax rate ranges from 40% to 46%.

Fee Simple: The whole ownership of property unburdened by any future interest or any possibility of losing total ownership. This is the highest form of property ownership. Other forms of property ownership are life estate, leasehold interest, or tenancy in common.

Fiduciary: Another name for a person appointed as a trustee, having the legal duty to act solely for the benefit of another.

Gift Tax Annual Exemption: Tax-free gifts may be made to any number of persons in a calendar year. Each tax-free gift made by a single individual may not exceed $14,000.00. Each tax-free gift made by a husband and wife may not exceed $28,000.00 per donee, per year. Gifts made in excess of the annual exemption are subject to federal gift tax in the year in which they are made.

Grantor: aka Trust Maker, Trustor, Settlor, the person who creates a trust.

Gross Value: The value of an estate before debts are paid. Probate fees are generally calculated on the gross value of the estate. For instance, if your estate consists of your residence with a market value of $150,000.00 and a mortgage of $100,000.00, probate fees would be based on the gross value of the estate before the mortgage is paid, which in this case would be $150,000.00.

Guardian: Someone who is legally responsible for the care of another person. A guardian is generally nominated in the case of a minor child in need of care or financial support, or when a person becomes disabled or incapable of caring for himself or herself. Guardians act under the supervision of a probate court and are responsible for all their actions to the court. See "Ward".

Heir: A person who would inherit property under state law, when a person dies without a will.

Holographic Will: This is a will entirely written, dated and signed by a person in his or her own handwriting. It is permitted only in a few states, often under very limited circumstances. Holographic wills should be avoided if at all possible.

Incapacitated or Incompetent: Someone who is unable to manage his or her own affairs either due to physical or mental impairment. An incompetent person cannot enter into a contract nor can he set up a trust, or appoint an agent to act in his behalf. In the absence of any planning for disability, a court will have to be petitioned for the appointment of a conservator guardian for an incompetent. Living Trust and Durable Powers of Attorney are tools for planning for legal incompetence to avoid court guardianships.

Income Beneficiary: A beneficiary who has a right to receive income of the trust, either presently or at some future time.

Intestate: A person who dies without a valid will.

Inter Vivos Trust: aka Living Trust, or Revocable Living Trust—A trust established by an individual during his or her lifetime, also known as a living trust. Such a trust can be either revocable or irrevocable.

Issue: All descendants of a particular person. The term includes children, grandchildren and other descendants.

Joint Tenancy with Right of Survivorship: Two or more persons that together hold the title with equal rights during their lifetime. The survivor will receive the entire property. In other words, death of a joint owner automatically transfers ownership of the property to the surviving joint tenants. Joint tenancy will overcome any provisions contained in a will. Joint tenancy has drawbacks and risks, and should only be used with legal advice. The consent of all joint tenants is necessary to sell, pledge, or encumber property owned in this fashion.

Life Estate: The right to use and enjoy property during the life of the individual who holds the property, with the property thereafter to go to someone else.

Lineal Descendants: Persons who are blood relatives.

Living Trust: aka Revocable Trust Living Trust—A trust established by an individual during his or her lifetime that can be changed or abolished. It is the most common Estate Planning design used today because it will avoid probate and taxes. Most importantly it will provide significant protections for the family after the Trust maker's passing.

Living Will: This is a written document containing instructions for a hospital or physician to allow a person to die a natural death without using artificial life-sustaining means after it is determined that the individual is terminally ill and there is no likelihood of recovery. This document should not be confused with a living trust. Each state has its own laws about Living Wills.

Minor: A child under the legal age to be considered an adult. Varies by state, usually under the age of 18 or 21. A minor cannot enter into a contract.

Multiple Probate: When a person dies who owned real property in more than one state, there must be separate probate court proceedings in each state where the real estate is located. If the title to the real property is held in a Revocable Living Trust, multiple probate estates in multiple states are avoided.

Net Value: The value of an estate after debts are paid. Federal estate taxes are based on the net value of the estate.

Perpetuities (Rule Against Perpetuities): A complex rule, the purpose of which is to keep property from being frozen in a will or trust beyond a certain period of time. This causes the trust to terminate automatically at the required time in order to protect the legality of the trust.

Personal Property: This is movable property such as furniture, automobiles, equipment, cash, and stock.

Pour-Over Will: A pour-over will is used to transfer property to a living trust after death if it was not already in a trust. People often fund their living trust with major assets they own. With a pour over will, any assets transferred to the trust after the trustor's death will have to go through probate. The advantage of the pour-over will is that it provides for a better disposition of your property under the provisions of one single instrument, namely the living trust.

Power of Attorney: This is a legal document giving another person, known as an agent or attorney in fact, the full legal authority to act in your behalf in case of your absence. Power of attorney may lose its validity if the principal becomes disabled and it is not valid after death. Most states however, permit a "durable" power of attorney, which remains valid through the disability or incompetence of the principal. A durable power of attorney can be used together with a living trust by allowing the agent to transfer any property into the trust that wasn't transferred prior to the trustor's death.

Principal: The assets of a trust and their proceeds, not to be confused with trust income, which is money earned by the assets held in trust.

Probate: The legal process that transfers a dead person's assets to his/her legal heirs. It is the process of administering a deceased person's estate. In the absence of a will, the probate court appoints an Administrator to handle a decedent's estate. All questions concerning the disposition and the rights of heirs and creditors are determined through probate. Probate is lengthy, costly, and open to the public. Assets are generally frozen or restricted during probate. Probate can be avoided if a good estate plan is created beforehand.

Probate Guardianship: A probate court appoints a guardian to manage the financial affairs of a disabled or incompetent person or the financial affairs of a minor child. The guardian is required to report their actions to the court.

Qualified Terminable Interest Property Trust (QTIP Trust): This is a special type of trust used mostly by married couples whose estate exceeds $5,340,000. The QTIP Trust allows the survivor to enjoy the income of the trust, but reserves the assets for the first deceased spouse's family or heirs and distributes the assets to them after the second spouse's death. Although it restricts the surviving spouse's use of the trust estate after the death of the first spouse, it defers estate taxes until after the second spouse's death.

Quit Claim Deed: A legal instrument used to release a person's right, title and interest in a piece of real property.

Real Property: Land and property permanently affixed to land, such as a house.

Real Estate: Same as real property.

Remaindermen: Those who receive trust assets or the "remainder" after the accomplishment of another purpose. The remaindermen have a future interest in the trust assets.

Revocable Trust: A trust that can be amended or terminated by its creator. As opposed to an irrevocable trust, a revocable trust is drafted to avoid taxes.

Settlor: Another name for a person who creates a trust.

Stepped-Up Basis: When a property is inherited, the person who inherits that property receives a new basis—monetary value—in the property. This is the stepped up basis—the value of the property at the date of the owner's death—which is usually more than the original worth of the property since property generally appreciates and increases its worth over time.

Tenancy In Common: Ownership of property by two or more persons. This is different from joint ownership or joint tenancy where upon the death of one person, all property is directly transferred to the other. In this case, upon the death of a tenant in common, ownership transfers to that person's heirs, not to the surviving owners.

Testamentary Trust: A trust that does not come into existence until after the testator's death.

Testator/Testatrix: The person who makes a will.

Trust: A document that enables an individual to manage property for the benefit of someone else and protects that property from taxes, creditors, and lawsuits.

Trustee: The person assigned to carry out the instructions of a trust and manage the property held in that trust.

Trust Protector: An individual besides the primary trustee who has the authority to make changes to a trust.

Trustor: The person who establishes a trust.

Unlimited Marital Deduction: Money or property left to a spouse free of federal estate taxes.

Ward: A person for whom a guardian is appointed.

Will Contest: A legal process that challenges the validity of a will.

Bibliography

1. Feiler, Bruce. "The Stories That Bind Us." *New York Times*. 17 Mar 2013: ST1. Print.
2. Sanders, Barrie. *Legacy: The Giving of Life's Greatest Treasures*. New York: Harper, 1999. Print.

Acknowledgements

I have been privileged to assist some of the greatest people in the world. I would like to thank all my clients who allowed me into their life. There is nothing better than finishing a project or a meeting and saying goodbye with a hug. My clients' challenges inspire me and I am grateful for the opportunity to help them through the most difficult times in their lives.

A big thank you goes out to Wendy Witt for helping me put all the legalese in my head on paper. Without her, this book would never have seen the light of day. Next, a thank you to Amy E. Jones for translating the legal gobbledygook in the glossary into something that anyone can understand. Randy Miller did a beautiful job of formatting this book and its companion, The Ultimate Estate Planning Guide.

Of course, I couldn't have done anything without the support of my terrific staff. I've had the privilege of working with Sandie Vedder, for almost 20 years. Not only is she a knowledgeable and dedicated paralegal, she is one of the finest people I know.

As for my daughter, Rachel, she believes that everyone who works for his/her father should be fired at least once. She left the office long enough to achieve a bachelor's degree in math and a Masters degree in math education, but thankfully, she keeps coming back to my office. She is a master at helping the clients and putting them at ease during some of the most difficult times in their lives.

My son Brian eventually worked his way up from his position as the office janitor to Chief of Information Technology and now creates all the online material for my company. He recently graduated from the University of Utah with a degree in business and I fear the day when he'll leave me to get a "real job" away from his father.

Dawn inherited the janitorial position, but has also become an excellent file clerk and expert scanner as she works towards becoming a writer. We all appreciate her efforts to make our facilities a more comfortable place to spend our days in.

Throughout the years all of my children have worked with me in my law office. Dillon took over as janitor from Brian. Tyler spent part of his years in college providing support in marketing and funding of trusts. Heather entered all the information in the document assembly program before she left for nursing school. Thanks goes to all my children who have all worked in my office

I had the privilege of working with my oldest son Ryan through college and for two years after he graduated until the day his life was cut short April 13, 2005. That one event influences everything I do with estate planning and estate settlements.

Finally, and most importantly, a mountain of thanks goes to my wife Joyce for sticking with me through this torturous process. She has given of her time and talents and endured more than one day of frustration balancing the books and keeping the business on track. Her expectation to see a finished project has helped push me through to the end.

About the Author

Larry Brock is an attorney entrepreneur who saw the high, the mighty, the low, and the mean all go through probate court in his law school days. He saw everything from multi-millionaire celebrity cases to poverty stricken estates as he lunched and dined with lawyers involved in every aspect of the business. He walked away from a lucrative litigation practice when tragedy struck his own family. Triggered by the senseless murder of his own son, Larry dedicated himself to helping clients protect themselves, their families, and their assets through comprehensive estate planning.

In addition to his traditional law firm, Larry has founded the **Academy of Online Estate Planning Attorneys,** through which individuals from across the nation get the best of both worlds: The convenience of working online and the counsel of an experienced and certified estate planning attorney who represents them and will let them know if they are headed in the wrong direction.

Larry's mission is to revolutionize the way estate planning legal services are delivered to individuals and families so that they are well prepared for the best of times, and the worst of times, as life unfolds.

Contact the Author

E. Lawrence Brock

Brock Law Office

193 S 100 E

St George, UT 84770

http://www.estateplandesigner.com

elb@brocklawoffice.com

Made in the USA
Monee, IL
08 November 2026

67971936R00046